# BROWN VOYAGE!

### THE BROWNIES ADVENTURES

## JAYDE, JAYSON & JAY'ELLE BROWN

B.R.O.W.N Voyage, LLC
Brownies Reaching Others With Narratives
Atlanta, Georgia USA

Copyright 2020 © Jayde Brown, Jay'Elle Brown & Jayson Brown.

Photo credits: Shawnta Necole & The Brown Family

All rights reserved. No part of this publication may be reproduced, distributed, or transmitted in any form or by any means, including photocopying, recording, or other electronic or mechanical methods, without the prior written permission of the publisher, except in the case of brief quotations embodied in critical reviews and certain other noncommercial uses permitted by copyright law.
Special discounts are available on quantity purchases by corporations, associations, and others. For details, contact the publisher or author.
Printed in the United States of America.
First Edition.

Library of Congress control number: 2020923374
ISBN: 978-1-7356195-0-7

www.BrownVoyage.com
thebrownvoyage@gmail.com
Facebook: @BrownVoyage
Instagram: @thebrownvoyage

## DEDICATION

*We dedicate this book to our grandparents and parents.
Thank you for your love and support.
We also dedicate this book to kids all around the world.
Let the world be your classroom!*

*~ the Brownies*

We are the Brownies and we are three siblings who love learning, exploring, trying new things, and most of all, traveling. In fact, we are known for taking 'schoolcations'; combining school with education.

Jayde is the travel researcher. It's good to research things, such as the weather, to know what kind of clothes to pack before you visit. You don't want to take summer clothes to a place where it's snowing! It's also good to research the currency so you know if you have to change your local money for theirs, the language so you can learn basic words, and even customs of a place before you go to make sure you respect the local culture.

This is Jayson, our travel photographer. Taking photos is a great way to share your trip with people and to look back and see
the places that you have been, the cultures you've experienced, and the people you have met.

This is Jay'Elle, our travel planner who helps create our itinerary. An itinerary is a schedule of events and activities that you follow to ensure you stay on track. This is very important especially if you have a limited time to visit or if you don't want to spend all day doing one thing.

Would you like to see some of the places that we have visited over the years? Come with us on a trip to some amazing places around the world. Ready? Set? Let's go!

# ENGLAND, UNITED KINGDOM

Buckingham Palace

The London Tube

Good day, mate and welcome to London, England. England is a part of the United Kingdom.

People in England speak English, and their national flag is called the Union Jack.

England is a monarchy, which means they have a royal family with a king or a queen. England's royal family lives in Buckingham Palace.

English people enjoy drinking tea and eating a pastry called crumpets. They also enjoy having fish and chips (potato fries). To get around in England, you can take a big double-decker bus. You can also ride the underground train, which is also called the Tube.

Some famous places in England are the London Bridge, the Big Ben bell tower, Buckingham Palace where the Queen of England lives, and the London Eye ferris wheel. We enjoyed watching the changing of the guards ceremony at the Buckingham Palace where on-duty guards are replaced with new guards.

# ITALY, EUROPE

The Vatican

*Ciao*, and welcome to Italy, a country which is on the continent of Europe. People in Italy speak Italian.

The country is known for many historical sites, including the Colosseum, the Leaning Tower of Pisa, the Sistine Chapel, and the Vatican, where the Pope lives.

Italy is also known for fashion and some of the most famous artists in the world.

Italian food is famous all over the world. Some foods invented in Italy are pasta, pizza, and gelato. Eating pizzas and gelatos at cafes was our favorite thing to do in Italy!

Trevi Fountain

Italian Pizza

The Colosseum

# FRANCE, EUROPE

*Eiffel Tower*

    *Bonjour*, and welcome to Paris, France.

    Paris is known as the city of love and is considered one of the most romantic places in the world. Many people travel to Paris for engagements, weddings and vow renewals. We were there when Mom and Dad celebrated their anniversary.

    Paris has many famous tourist attractions, like the Eiffel Tower, Louvre Museum, Notre Dame Cathedral, the Arc de Triomphe, and many palaces from the time the country had kings and queens.

    The French are known for their cuisine, which includes foods like escargot, croissants, truffles, crepes, macaroons, baguettes, and ratatouille.

# JAPAN, ASIA

Kon'nichiwa, and welcome to Tokyo, a city in Japan, which is in Asia.

The language spoken there is Japanese. Japan is known for seafood, and it is the place where sushi was invented.

Japan is also well known for being a very technologically advanced city.

Tokyo is known for beautiful cherry blossom trees and festivals in the spring.

Tokyo is also known for the Tokyo Tower and beautiful temples and shrines.
We got to go up 250 meters, to the top observatory deck of the Tokyo Tower, and enjoyed a beautiful panoramic view of the city! The Tokyo Tower's also a radio tower for TV and radio stations.

The Japanese people created many martial art forms, including karate, jujutsu, sumo wrestling, and judo.

# PERU, SOUTH AMERICA

*Bienvenidos* to Peru, which is the third largest country in South America.

Peruvians speak Spanish and Quechua, and their local money is called Nuevo Sol.

Peru is home to the Amazon, the largest rainforest in the world, as well as the Andes Mountains, the world's second highest mountain range.

There are ancient temples and remains of cities which were built by the Incas, the original people of Peru.

Peru is known for its llamas, alpacas, and even a colony of penguins.

Peru is also known for The Parque del Amor (Park of Love) with a giant, kissing sculpture overlooking the southeast Pacific Ocean. We enjoyed eating churros, which are sweet and crunchy pastries, popular all over Peru. We also got to learn about the Peruvian government at the Government Palace.

*Park of Love*

# SOUTH AFRICA

*Constitution Court*

Hello, and welcome to South Africa, the southernmost country on the continent of Africa. The capital is Johannesburg.

There are people from many cultures here, so much so that there are eleven official languages spoken in South Africa, including English, Zulu, Afrikaan, and Xhosa.

South African currency is called the rand. South Africa has many wild animals like antelope, elephants, lions, hippopotamus, giraffes, and more that you can see on safaris.

A famous, natural site is Tugela Falls, the world's second tallest waterfall. Nelson Mandela is one of the most famous South Africans. Mahatma Gandhi also lived there during his life. They were jailed in the same prison at Constitution Hill.

Mandela was an important figure in helping to end segregation, also known as apartheid. We got to learn about the country's fight for democracy at Constitution Hill.

# EGYPT, AFRICA

*The Great Pyramids of Giza & The Sphinx*

Egypt is a country in northeast Africa and is home to the longest river in the world, the Nile. The Nile is the primary source of Egypt's water.

Even though the Nile is in Egypt, it is a country that is very dry with both the Sahara and Libyan Desert. Egypt has lots of wildlife, including gazelles, crocodiles, and cobras.

Egypt is known for its ancient history and structures, built thousands of years ago, such as the Great Pyramid of Giza and the Sphinx, which are still standing.

Many believe Egyptians invented paper by using papyrus plants. We did a tour and learned how papyrus is made. The country is also known for its rich artifacts from the Pharaohs (kings) tombs and mummies, which have been displayed all over the world.

# COSTA RICA, SOUTH AMERICA

Hola, and welcome to Costa Rica. It is in Central America with the Caribbean Sea on one side and the Pacific Ocean on the other. The country has mountains and many volcanoes.

Although Spanish is the main language spoken, many people also speak English. The currency used in Costa Rica is the colon.

While there are monkeys, jaguars, and lots of colorful wild birds like the macaw, Costa Rica's most unique animal is the sloth.

Rice and beans are popular ingredients in lots of Costa Rican dishes, like casado, as well as gallo pinto. Coffee Plantations are popular all over Costa Rica. Our family enjoyed learning the history and the process of making coffee in Costa Rica.

# ISRAEL, MIDDLE EAST

*The Dead Sea*

Shalom, and welcome to Israel, a country in the Middle East. Most people in Israel speak Hebrew or Arabic, and their currency is called shekels.

Israel is well known for its history, religious sites, and for having Bible connections to Jesus.

The city of Jericho, the oldest inhabited city in the world, is also located here. We rode a cable car up to the top of Mount Temptation in Jericho.

The country is also known for the Jordan River and the Dead Sea, which is so salty, no plants or animals are able to live in it. After the Jewish Holocaust in Europe, many survivors resettled in Israel.

A famous dish in Israel is hummus, a dip made from chickpeas.

Jericho

Sheckels

# CANADA, NORTH AMERICA

## Niagara Falls

Canada is a country in North America and the second largest country in the world in terms of land mass.

A portion of Canada is in the Artic Ocean. English and French are both recognized as the official languages.

Canada has about twenty percent of the world's fresh water and over three million lakes.

A popular natural attraction in Canada is Niagara Falls. We rode a boat to the falls! A popular sport in Canada is ice hockey.

# JAMAICA, CARIBBEAN

Wah gwaan, and welcome to Jamaica, an island in the Caribbean. The official language of Jamaica is English, even though most people speak patois (local dialect).

Jamaica has natural attractions such as the Spice Mountains, beaches, and the Dunn's River waterfall. Local food include patties, jerk chicken, callaloo, ackee, and fish.

Jamaica is also the birthplace of reggae music, made famous by Bob Marley. We got to tour the historic Rose Hall Great House and learned about the lifestyle of the European middle class in the isles of the Caribbean in the Eighteenth Century.

While in Jamaica, our family also got to visit a local school and meet local students.

# BELGIUM, EUROPE

*Grand Place of Brussels*

Belgium is a country in Europe. While French is mostly spoken, many people also speak Flemish, which is similar to Dutch.

The country is known for chocolates, Belgium waffles, and in the capital city of Brussels, Brussel sprouts were created.

One of the most popular tourist attractions is Grand Place, which was started in the 10th century as a fort and market. It was an important site in Belgium history for many things, including government activities.

Nowadays, Grand Place is especially active during the holidays. In Belgium, we enjoyed learning the process of making chocolate at a chocolate factory and eating Belgian waffles.

Grand Place of Brussels

Belgian Waffles and hot cocoa

# Comprehension Check

What is the underground train in London called?

What country is known for the Colosseum and the Vatican?

What famous foods is Paris, France known for?

What kind of trees are famous all over Tokyo in the springtime?

What is the third largest county in South America?

Which country has 11 official languages?

Where can the Nile River and Sahara Desert be found?

What is Costa Rica well known for?

What is the name of the sea that is so salty, there is no plant or animal life?

What is the name of the giant waterfalls in Toronto, Canada?

What country is the birthplace of Bob Marley?

What sweet treats is Belgium known for?

# Write About it!
Narrative Writing (state three supporting claims)

## Which country do you want to visit and why?

_____
_____
_____
_____
_____
_____
_____
_____
_____
_____
_____
_____
_____
_____

# Non-Fiction Notes
taking notes can help you remember what you read

## Important words to know

## questions I still have

# Author's Purpose
## every author has a reason for writing!

What main idea did the authors want to share?
_____
_____
_____
_____
_____
_____

What thoughts or feelings do the authors want you to have?
_____
_____
_____
_____
_____
_____

# Fact or Opinion
### find examples of facts and opinions from the book

## Share five facts from this book

**1** _____

**2** _____

**3** _____

**4** _____

**5** _____

**FACTS ARE PIECES OF INFORMATION THAT CAN BE PROVEN.**

**OPINIONS SHOW HOW SOMEONE FEELS ABOUT SOMETHING.**

### Share one opinion of your favorite country from this book.

_____

_____

# Compare and Contrast

Write one country in each circle. Write facts about the countries in the circle. In the center, write what the two countries have in common.

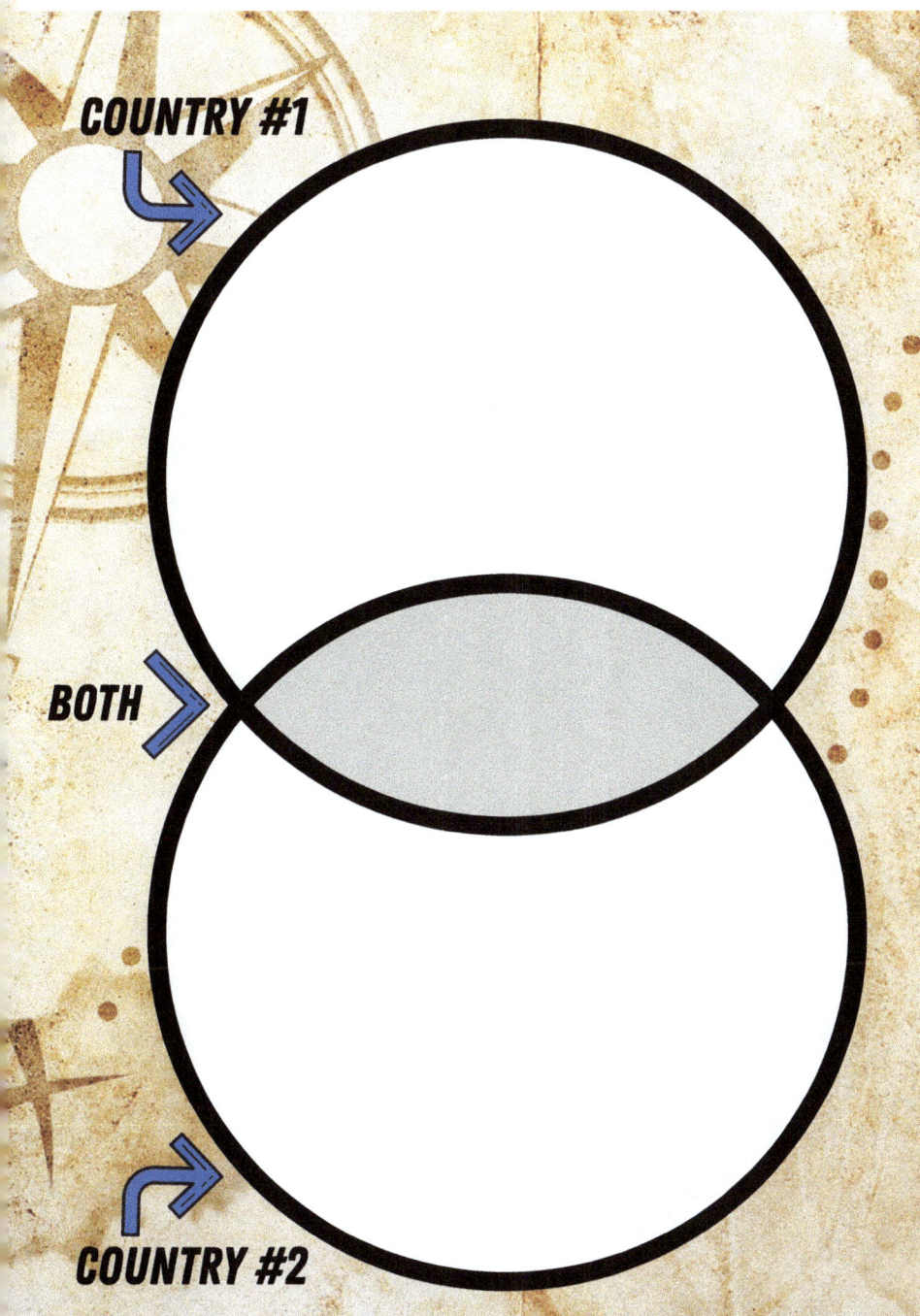

COUNTRY #1

BOTH

COUNTRY #2

# About the Authors

Born and raised in Decatur, Georgia, USA Jayson, Jayde and Jay'Elle Brown all share a love of traveling, instilled in them by their parents Jayson and Tammy.

As of 2020, the siblings traveled to 5 of the 7 continents. The Brownies, as they are affectionately called, have four Pomeranian pups, all named after places they've visited - Paris, London, Bali, and Johannesburg (JoJo for short).

In addition to traveling, all three of the Brownies are rising talents on the Atlanta acting scene, having worked as actors on season one of *Lovecraft Country*, *The Underground*, *Thunder Force*, *Coming 2 America*, as well as independent films, and in music videos for award-winning artists.

Jayson is the oldest of the three, born in 2006. He enjoys traveling, performing arts, and playing the drums. He is a percussionist who plays in his school band. He also trained with the Atlanta Drum Academy and performed with them for Superbowl LIII Live Concert hosted by Jermaine Dupree. Jayson is also an aspiring entrepreneur.

Jay'Elle is the middle child in the family, and she enjoys singing and performing arts. She is a member of her school's drama club and will appear in several upcoming projects. She's also a kidprenuer who launched her company BXtra by Jay'Elle at 12. Through her online boutique, www.bxtrajayelle.com, she sells homemade vegan beauty products like lip gloss, edge control, and apparel promoting positivity and empowerment for girls. Jay'Elle enjoys exploring cultures, mingling with locals, and she has done school visits in Jamaica where she donated health supplies and her lip gloss to girls.

The youngest of the Brownies, Jayde, was born in 2009. She attends a performing arts academy where she majors in dance. She also enjoys drawing and loves looking at artwork in museums around the world. Jayde wants to be a professional ballerina and perform around the world! She, too, is an aspiring entrepreneur.

For more information visit www.brownvoyage.com

www.ingramcontent.com/pod-product-compliance
Lightning Source LLC
Chambersburg PA
CBHW070134100426
42744CB00009B/1840